JOB Smarts

12 Steps to Job Success

Second Edition

Activities to help you find, get, and keep a job!

by Dixie Lee Wright

Works

America's Career Publisher

Job Smarts, Second Edition
12 Steps to Job Success

Previous edition was titled *Know-How Is the Key: 12 Steps to Job Success.*

© 2004 by Dixie Lee Wright

Published by JIST Works, an imprint of JIST Publishing, Inc.
8902 Otis Avenue
Indianapolis, IN 46216-1033

Phone: 1-800-648-JIST   Fax: 1-800-JIST-FAX
E-mail: info@jist.com   Web site: www.jist.com

Note to instructors. Support material is available for *Job Smarts,* Second Edition. An essential instructor's guide contains helpful guidance for teaching classes and many activities and assignments. Call 1-800-648-JIST for details.

About career materials published by JIST: Our materials encourage people to be self-directed and to take control of their destinies. We work hard to provide excellent content, solid advice, and techniques that get results. If you have questions about this book or other JIST products, call 1-800-648-JIST or visit www.jist.com.

Quantity discounts are available for JIST products. Please call 1-800-648-JIST or visit www.jist.com for a free catalog and more information.

Visit www.jist.com for information on JIST, free job search information, book excerpts, and ordering information on our many products. For free information on 14,000 job titles, visit www.careeroink.com.

Also by Dixie Lee Wright:

Job Survival: How to Adjust and Keep Your Job

Acquisitions Editor: Randy Haubner
Development Editor: Stephanie Koutek
Cover Designer: Aleata Howard
Interior Designer: Trudy Coler
Interior Layout: Debra Kincaid
Proofreader: Jeanne Clark

Printed in the United States of America

07 06 05   9 8 7 6 5 4 3 2

ISBN 1-59357-028-7

About This Book

The worksheets in this book will help teach you how to find, get, and keep a job. Your instructor will assign them in class and as homework. You'll do many different kinds of activities designed to help you in your job search—word scrambles and matching, filling in blanks, choosing which items you like the best, and writing stories and ads about yourself and others.

You'll also learn how to discover what you like and what kinds of jobs you can do with your skills. The book will help you through finding job openings, writing a resume and cover letter, and filling out applications. You'll find out what causes people to get fired, what good teamwork is like, and how to make a good impression during an interview.

Good luck with your new job!

Table of Contents

Worksheet #1

My Principles, Interests, and Skills

Principles

My friends say I am

_____

_____

_____

Interests

My friends say I like to

_____

_____

_____

Skills

My friends say I can do

_____

_____

_____

My Six Power Words

1. _____

2. _____

3. _____

4. _____

5. _____

6. _____

Worksheet #2

Identifying Principles

Things I Would Not Do/Things I Might Do

Read the following list. Print an N in the blank next to things you would not do. Print an M in the blank next to things you might do.

_____ Walk away from an accident	_____ Deny a mistake
_____ Report someone for stealing	_____ Lie on an application
_____ Make excuses for not showing up	_____ Walk out at work
_____ Make fun of people	_____ Steal money
_____ Hit someone at work	_____ Eat on the job
_____ Visit with friends at work	_____ Do drugs
_____ Take something from work	_____ Drink alcohol
_____ Make long-distance phone calls from work	_____ Repeat gossip
_____ Punch a time card for a friend	_____ Take many breaks
_____ Take money from the cash register	_____ Tell on a friend
_____ Pretend to read well	_____ Break a promise
_____ Tell lies about a co-worker	_____ Tell a secret
	_____ Cuss someone out
	_____ Fake being sick

Count your Ns. These are your *principles.*

Worksheet #3

Power Words

Increase Your Vocabulary

Look at the list below. What do these words say about someone? Next to each word, write a few words describing what it means.

Word	What does it say?
Loyal	Supportive of others
Trustworthy	Can be trusted
Punctual	Always on time
Compassionate	_____
Truthful	_____
Considerate	_____
Reliable	_____
Humorous	_____
Non-judgmental	_____
Loving	_____
Drug-free	_____
Open-minded	_____
Kind	_____
Practical	_____
Straightforward	_____
Sincere	_____
Consistent	_____
Ambitious	_____
Energetic	_____

If you were the hiring manager for a company, which two words would impress you the most? Circle those two words.

Do either or both of the two words describe you?   Yes   No

Worksheet #4

My Interests

Read the following list of interests and circle what you think is fun:

Watching TV	Music
Using the VCR	Movies
Shopping	Sending e-mail
Using a computer	Sports
Art	Reading
Puzzles	Cars
Motors	Cooking
Baking	Cleaning
Makeup	Gardening
Looking at Web sites	Sightseeing
Concerts	Animals
Family	Church
Camping	Holiday gatherings
Acting	Singing
Dancing	Plants

Worksheet #5

Identifying Personality Types

Decide whether an outgoing person or a private person would be more likely to enjoy the following activities. Write an O for outgoing or a P for private in the blank before each activity.

_____ Fishing alone

_____ Joining a motorcycle club

_____ Going to a public swimming pool

_____ Hiking with friends

_____ Dancing at a club

_____ Reading non-fiction

_____ Writing stories

_____ Playing basketball

_____ Playing volleyball

_____ Watching baseball

_____ Drawing nature pictures

_____ Making crafts

_____ Gardening

_____ Stamp collecting

_____ Singing in a choir

_____ Going to church groups

_____ Attending big parties

_____ Playing video games

_____ Group rafting

_____ Going to small family picnics

_____ Going to block barbeques

_____ Searching the Internet

_____ Fixing cars

_____ Watching car races

_____ Watching TV shows about history

Look at the list. Are you a outgoing or private person? Circle one.

Outgoing   Private

Write two of your interests on the lines below. Next to each one, write a job that relates to it.

1. _____

2. _____

Worksheet #6

My Skills

Read the following list of skills and circle what you think you can do:

Read	Dance
Write	Sing
Draw	Play an instrument
Cook	Read music
Sew	Assemble things
Add numbers	Give customer service
Use the telephone	Run
Paint	Skate
Clean	Play basketball
Baby-sit	Play volleyball
Build things	Ride a bike
Cut the lawn	Other: _____
Fix motors	Other: _____
Use a computer	Other: _____

Worksheet #7

Job Skills

You need to know the skills you have, but you also need to know what skills certain jobs require.

Sometimes we hear about jobs we would like to try, but we have no idea what skills it takes to do the job.

Everyone has to start somewhere. Usually, people start out in an entry-level job.

Look at the following list and choose two jobs you would like to try.

Car washer	Theatre ticket taker	Nursery school aide
Server	Lobby attendant	Drywall worker
Hotel housekeeper	Dry cleaner attendant	Hotel porter
Stocking clerk	Receptionist	Assembly line
Janitorial	Pizza maker	Retail clerk
Florist helper	Telemarketer	Data entry
Line cook	File clerk	Shampoo attendant
Cafeteria server	Parking attendant	Cart retriever
Carpet cleaner	Teacher's aide	Hairdresser
Construction cleanup	Lawn worker	Manicurist

Write the names of the two jobs you chose here:

_____

List the skills you think are needed to do each job on the lines below.

_____

_____

Do you have those skills?

_____

_____

Can you acquire those skills with your special needs?

_____

_____

Worksheet #8

Setting Goals for Me

I Like Me

Name: _____

I See Me

Name: _____

_____

_____

_____

_____

_____

I Can See Me Doing These Three Jobs:

_____

_____

_____

_____

_____

Worksheet #9

Writing Short- and Long-Term Job Goals

Short-term goals last for six to twelve months, and long-term goals last as long as five years into the future. In the spaces below, write some job-related goals that you want to accomplish in that time.

6 months

_____

_____

_____

_____

12 months

_____

_____

_____

_____

5 years

_____

_____

_____

_____

Worksheet #10

Choosing Short-Term Life Goals

A short-term goal lasts from six months to a year.

Many things in life come with a price tag. Which things on this list are you willing to work for a year to accomplish? Circle those things.

Stereo _____   Trade school _____

New TV _____   Short vacation _____

Used car _____   DVD player _____

Own apartment _____   Checking account_____

Engagement _____   Jewelry _____

Furniture _____   Clothes _____

Savings account _____   Sporting equipment _____

Camera _____   Other: _____

Speed bike_____   Other: _____

Community college _____   Other: _____

Now, consider the cost of the items you have chosen. Are you willing to pay the price? Put a price tag beside three of your choices.

Worksheet #11

Choosing Long-Term Life Goals

A long-term goal lasts three to five years.

Some items come with a higher price tag. Are you willing to work for three to five years to pay the price? Circle the items that you would work for three to five years to gain.

Own house or condo _____   Exercise equipment _____

Get married _____   Jewelry _____

New car _____   Motorcycle _____

Children _____   Leisure recreation _____

Four-year college _____   Health club _____

Time-share _____   Stocks _____

Camper _____   Bonds _____

Cruise _____   Other: _____

Digital camera _____   Other: _____

Big wedding _____   Other: _____

Travel _____

Now, put a price tag beside three of your pricier choices.

Worksheet #12

Your Attitude Is Showing

Negative feelings

Things that tick me off:

_____

_____

_____

_____

Words that tick me off:

_____

_____

_____

_____

Positive feelings

Things that make me feel good:

_____

_____

_____

_____

Words that make me feel good:

_____

_____

_____

_____

Worksheet #13

Make a Quick Fix

How to Overcome Negative Words and Bad Feelings

- ✔ Walk away from the situation
- ✔ Take deep breaths and try to relax
- ✔ Take a break and do something else
- ✔ Sing or hum a happy song
- ✔ Change the topic of conversation
- ✔ Tell a funny story
- ✔ Compliment someone or something
- ✔ Talk to yourself in the mirror
- ✔ Walk outside—yell if you must

How to Hold On to Positive Words and Feelings

- ✔ Repeat your positive words
- ✔ Compliment the person you are talking to
- ✔ Sing or hum a happy song
- ✔ Remember positive words
- ✔ Hold positive thoughts
- ✔ Think of something funny
- ✔ Take credit for your feelings
- ✔ Talk to yourself in the mirror
- ✔ Walk outside—yell if you must

Worksheet #14

Attitudes

Look at the list of behaviors below. If you think the behavior is positive, put a P in the space next to it. If you think the behavior is negative, put an N.

_____ Always helping co-workers

_____ Saying "I told you so"

_____ Complimenting co-workers

_____ Being critical of co-workers

_____ Having a good sense of humor

_____ Being hard to put up with

_____ Not being critical of the boss

_____ Being a good team player

_____ Promoting doubt about the team

_____ Trying to show both sides of a problem

_____ Trying to make the boss look good

_____ Working to improve profit

_____ Being careless at work

_____ Discouraging co-workers

_____ Encouraging co-workers

_____ Gossiping about co-workers

_____ Showing prejudice against ethnic groups

Which kind of person would you rather work with?	Negative	Positive
Which kind of person would you rather have as an employee?	Negative	Positive
Which kind of person would you rather have as a friend?	Negative	Positive
Which kind of person has a better attitude?	Negative	Positive

Think about your behavior. Is your attitude negative or positive? Is it good for you?

_____

_____

Worksheet #15

I Shall Overcome

My Personal Barriers

_____
_____
_____
_____
_____
_____

Ways to Overcome My Personal Barriers

_____
_____
_____
_____
_____
_____
_____
_____

Worksheet #16

Worksite Barriers

Sometimes your co-workers may act differently around you. Next to each action below, write something you can do to help the co-worker get to know you and become more comfortable around you.

Co-worker's Actions   **What Can I Do?**

Lack of conversation _____

Refuses to sit by me _____

Never says "Good morning" _____

Jokes with everyone but me _____

Offers food to others but not me _____

Makes facial expressions imitating me _____

Makes remarks about me _____

Assumptions

Write your first thought about these people in the blank space on the right.

Person who uses a wheelchair _____

Janitor _____

Preacher _____

Lawyer _____

Male ballet dancer _____

Motorcyclist _____

Doctor _____

Truck driver _____

Hispanic person _____

Asian person _____

Male hairdresser _____

Stripper _____

Garbage truck operator _____

Female construction worker _____

Ditch digger _____

Person who is blind _____

Mechanic _____

Felon _____

Worksheet #17

First Jobs After Graduation

1. _____

2. _____

3. _____

Worksheet #18

Pre-Resume Worksheet

The resume needs to answer these questions for the employer:

Who are you?

Your full name: _____

Your street address: _____

Your city, state, and ZIP code: _____

Your full telephone number: _____

Your job objective

What do you want to do?

_____

_____

_____

Special skills

What can you do?

_____

_____

Strengths

What is the best thing about you?

_____

_____

Accomplishments

What have you done that you are proud of?

_____

_____

Employment history

Job title/position: _____

Name of employer: _____

Address of employer: _____

Years you were employed: _____

What did you do on your job? _____

_____

_____

_____

Education

Certificate or degree you earned: _____

Name and location of school: _____

Year you graduated: _____

References

Name: _____

Address: _____

Telephone number: _____

Name: _____

Address: _____

Telephone number: _____

Name: _____

Address: _____

Telephone number: _____

Worksheet #19

Functional Resume Format

Your Name
Street Address
City, State, and ZIP Code
Telephone Number

Job Objective:

Special Skills:

Personal Accomplishments:

Work History:
    Company:
    Address:
    Dates employed:
    Job title:

    Company:
    Address:
    Dates employed:
    Job title:

Education:
    School name, city, and state
    Date of graduation
    Certificate or degree earned

References available upon request.

Worksheet #20

Words That Describe Me

Circle any word that describes who you are and what you have done.

Team player	Good marketing
Cautious	Outgoing
Safety-minded	Profit-focused
Accurate	Computer knowledge
Leadership	Good budgeting
Customer satisfaction	Following directions
Increased sales	Accounting
Led workshops	Physically fit
Analytical	Cheerful
Creative	Kind
Decision-making	Respectful
Time management	Work-oriented
Problem-solving	Goal setter
Energetic	Achiever
Results-driven	Responsible

Worksheet #21

Cover Letter Format

Your name
Your address
City, state, ZIP code
Date

Name of addressee, title
Company name
Company address
City, state, ZIP code

Dear Mr./Ms.:

Paragraph 1: Explain why you are writing and where you received the job lead.

Paragraph 2: Advertise your resume.

Paragraph 3: Set the possible interview.

Sincerely,

Your signature

Printed Name

Enc.: Resume

Worksheet #22

Your Success Story

Example

Joe's church group was trying to raise money so they could go to youth camp. They decided to sell advanced tickets for a car wash on a certain weekend. Each member of the group would have to sell a certain number of tickets and work an allotted block of time to qualify for a discounted group rate. Selling the tickets was no problem; however, Nick, one of the other members, had a heart condition. The weather was very hot that weekend and Nick could not work his block of time.

Joe volunteered to work his block as well as Nick's block so they could both qualify for the discount price for youth camp.

What did Joe do to make this a success story?

1. _____

2. _____

3. _____

What three words could Joe use to describe himself?

_____

What three words would impress an employer?

_____

Write your own success story:

_____

_____

_____

What three words describe you?

_____

What three words would impress an employer?

_____

Worksheet #23
Application for Employment

Name: _____

APPLICATION FOR EMPLOYMENT

We are an equal opportunity employer, dedicated to a policy of nondiscrimination in employment on any basis, including race, color, age, sex, religion, handicap, or national origin.

PERSONAL INFORMATION

Date _____ Social Security Number _____

Name _____
         Last   First   Middle

Present address _____
                  Street   City   State   Zip

Permanent address _____
                    Street   City   State   Zip

Phone no. _____

Referred by _____ Are you 18 years of age or older? ❑ Yes ❑ No

EMPLOYMENT DESIRED

Position _____ Date you can start _____ Salary desired _____

Are you employed now? ❑ Yes ❑ No   If so, may we inquire of your present employer? ❑ Yes ❑ No

Have you applied to this company before? ❑ Yes ❑ No   Where? _____   When? _____

EDUCATION

	Name and location of school	Circle last year completed	Did you graduate?	Subjects studied and degree(s) received
Grammar school			❑ Yes ❑ No	
High school		1 2 3 4	❑ Yes ❑ No	
College		1 2 3 4	❑ Yes ❑ No	
Trade, business, or correspondence school		1 2 3 4	❑ Yes ❑ No	

GENERAL

Subjects of special study or research work _____

Job-related skills (typing, driver's license, etc.) _____

Activities other than religious (civic, athletic, etc.) _____

Exclude organizations, the name or character of which indicated the race, sex, color, or national origin of its members

FORMER EMPLOYERS   List below your last four employers, starting with the last one first.

Date mo./year	Name and address of employer	Salary (upon leaving)	Position	Reason for leaving
From To				
From To				
From To				
From To				

REFERENCES   List below three persons not related to you, whom you have known at least one year.

	Name	Address	Position	Years Acquainted
1				
2				
3				

AUTHORIZATION

I authorize investigation of all statements contained in this application. I understand that misrepresentation of information requested is cause for dismissal. Further, I understand and agree that my employment is for no definite period and may, regardless of the date of payment of my wages and salary, be terminated at any time without cause and without any previous notice.

Date _____   Signature _____

In case of emergency notify _____
                                                        Name

_____
Address   Phone no.

_____

DO NOT WRITE BELOW THIS LINE—OFFICE USE ONLY

Interviewed by _____   Date _____

Remarks: _____

_____

S Form I-9 completed? ❏ Yes ❏ No _____

ed _____ For dept. _____ Position _____ Will report _____ Salary/wages _____

oved: 1. _____   2. _____   3. _____
            Employment manager   Dept. head   General manager

Worksheet #24

Employee's Withholding Allowance Certificate Form W-4

Form W-4 (2003)

Purpose. Complete Form W-4 so that your employer can withhold the correct Federal income tax from your pay. Because your tax situation may change, you may want to refigure your withholding each year.

Exemption from withholding. If you are exempt, complete only lines 1, 2, 3, 4, and 7 and sign the form to validate it. Your exemption for 2003 expires February 16, 2004. See Pub. 505, Tax Withholding and Estimated Tax.

Note: *You cannot claim exemption from withholding if:* **(a)** *your income exceeds $750 and includes more than $250 of unearned income (e.g., interest and dividends) and* **(b)** *another person can claim you as a dependent on their tax return.*

Basic instructions. If you are not exempt, complete the **Personal Allowances Worksheet** below. The worksheets on page 2 adjust your withholding allowances based on itemized deductions, certain credits, adjustments to income, or two-earner/two-job situations. Complete all worksheets that apply. However, you **may claim fewer (or zero) allowances.**

Head of household. Generally, you may claim head of household filing status on your tax return only if you are unmarried and pay more than 50% of the costs of keeping up a home for yourself and your dependent(s) or other qualifying individuals. See line E below.

Tax credits. You can take projected tax credits into account in figuring your allowable number of withholding allowances. Credits for child or dependent care expenses and the child tax credit may be claimed using the **Personal Allowances Worksheet** below. See Pub. 919, How Do I Adjust My Tax Withholding? for information on converting your other credits into withholding allowances.

Nonwage income. If you have a large amount of nonwage income, such as interest or dividends, consider making estimated tax payments using Form 1040-ES, Estimated Tax for Individuals. Otherwise, you may owe additional tax.

Two earners/two jobs. If you have a working spouse or more than one job, figure the total number of allowances you are entitled to claim on all jobs using worksheets from only one Form W-4. Your withholding usually will be most accurate when all allowances are claimed on the Form W-4 for the highest paying job and zero allowances are claimed on the others.

Nonresident alien. If you are a nonresident alien, see the **Instructions for Form 8233** before completing this Form W-4.

Check your withholding. After your Form W-4 takes effect, use Pub. 919 to see how the dollar amount you are having withheld compares to your projected total tax for 2003. See Pub. 919, especially if your earnings exceed $125,000 (Single) or $175,000 (Married).

Recent name change? If your name on line 1 differs from that shown on your social security card, call 1-800-772-1213 for a new social security card.

Personal Allowances Worksheet (Keep for your records.)

A Enter "1" for **yourself** if no one else can claim you as a dependent . . . . **A** _____

B Enter "1" if: {
- You are single and have only one job; or
- You are married, have only one job, and your spouse does not work; or
- Your wages from a second job or your spouse's wages (or the total of both) are $1,000 or less.
} . . **B** _____

C Enter "1" for your **spouse.** But, you may choose to enter "-0-" if you are married and have either a working spouse or more than one job. (Entering "-0-" may help you avoid having too little tax withheld.) . . . . **C** _____

D Enter number of **dependents** (other than your spouse or yourself) you will claim on your tax return . . . . **D** _____

E Enter "1" if you will file as **head of household** on your tax return (see conditions under **Head of household** above) . **E** _____

F Enter "1" if you have at least $1,500 of **child or dependent care expenses** for which you plan to claim a credit . . **F** _____
(**Note:** Do **not** include child support payments. See **Pub. 503**, *Child and Dependent Care Expenses*, for details.)

G **Child Tax Credit** (including additional child tax credit):
- If your total income will be between $15,000 and $42,000 ($20,000 and $65,000 if married), enter "1" for each eligible child plus **1 additional** if you have three to five eligible children or **2 additional** if you have six or more eligible children.
- If your total income will be between $42,000 and $80,000 ($65,000 and $115,000 if married), enter "1" if you have one or two eligible children, "2" if you have three eligible children, "3" if you have four eligible children, or "4" if you have five or more eligible children. . . . . . **G** _____

H Add lines A through G and enter total here. **Note:** *This may be different from the number of exemptions you claim on your tax return.* ▶ **H** _____

For accuracy, complete all worksheets that apply.
- If you plan to **itemize or claim adjustments to income** and want to reduce your withholding, see the **Deductions and Adjustments Worksheet** on page 2.
- If you have **more than one job** or are **married and you and your spouse both work** and the combined earnings from all jobs exceed $35,000, see the **Two-Earner/Two-Job Worksheet** on page 2 to avoid having too little tax withheld.
- If **neither** of the above situations applies, **stop here** and enter the number from line H on line 5 of Form W-4 below.

- - - - - - - - - - - - - - - - **Cut here and give Form W-4 to your employer. Keep the top part for your records.** - - - - - - - - - - - - - - - -

Form **W-4**
Department of the Treasury
Internal Revenue Service

Employee's Withholding Allowance Certificate

▶ **For Privacy Act and Paperwork Reduction Act Notice, see page 2.**

OMB No. 1545-0010

2003

1 Type or print your first name and middle initial	Last name		2 Your social security number

Home address (number and street or rural route)

City or town, state, and ZIP code

3 ☐ Single ☐ Married ☐ Married, but withhold at higher Sin
Note: *If married, but legally separated, or spouse is a nonresident alien, check the*

4 If your last name differs from that shown on your social card, check here. You must call 1-800-772-1213 for a ne

5 Total number of allowances you are claiming (from line H above **or** from the applicable worksheet on page 2) **5**

6 Additional amount, if any, you want withheld from each paycheck **6**

7 I claim exemption from withholding for 2003, and I certify that I meet **both** of the following conditions for exemption
- Last year I had a right to a refund of **all** Federal income tax withheld because I had **no** tax liability **and**
- This year I expect a refund of **all** Federal income tax withheld because I expect to have **no** tax liability.
If you meet both conditions, write "Exempt" here . . . . ▶ **7**

Under penalties of perjury, I certify that I am entitled to the number of withholding allowances claimed on this certificate, or I am entitled to
Employee's signature
(Form is not valid unless you sign it.) ▶

Date ▶

8 Employer's name and address (Employer: Complete lines 8 and 10 only if sending to the IRS.) | **9** Office code (optional) | **10** Em

Cat. No. 10220Q

Worksheet #25

Immigration Form I-9

U.S. Department of Justice
Immigration and Naturalization Service

OMB No. 1115-0136

Employment Eligibility Verification

Please read instructions carefully before completing this form. The instructions must be available during completion of this form. ANTI-DISCRIMINATION NOTICE: It is illegal to discriminate against work eligible individuals. Employers CANNOT specify which document(s) they will accept from an employee. The refusal to hire an individual because of a future expiration date may also constitute illegal discrimination.

Section 1. Employee Information and Verification. To be completed and signed by employee at the time employment begins.

Print Name: Last	First	Middle Initial	Maiden Name
Address *(Street Name and Number)*		Apt. #	Date of Birth *(month/day/year)*
City	State	Zip Code	Social Security #

I am aware that federal law provides for imprisonment and/or fines for false statements or use of false documents in connection with the completion of this form.

I attest, under penalty of perjury, that I am (check one of the following):

☐ A citizen or national of the United States
☐ A Lawful Permanent Resident (Alien # A_____)
☐ An alien authorized to work until ___/___/___
(Alien # or Admission #) _____

Employee's Signature

Date *(month/day/year)*

Preparer and/or Translator Certification. *(To be completed and signed if Section 1 is prepared by a person other than the employee.) I attest, under penalty of perjury, that I have assisted in the completion of this form and that to the best of my knowledge the information is true and correct.*

Preparer's/Translator's Signature	Print Name
Address *(Street Name and Number, City, State, Zip Code)*	Date *(month/day/year)*

Section 2. Employer Review and Verification. To be completed and signed by employer. Examine one document from List A OR examine one document from List B and one from List C, as listed on the reverse of this form, and record the title, number and expiration date, if any, of the document(s)

List A	OR	List B	AND	List C
Document title: _____		_____		_____
Issuing authority: _____		_____		_____
Document #: _____		_____		_____
Expiration Date *(if any):* ___/___/___		___/___/___		___/___/___
Document #: _____				
Expiration Date *(if any):* ___/___/___				

CERTIFICATION - I attest, under penalty of perjury, that I have examined the document(s) presented by the above-named employee, that the above-listed document(s) appear to be genuine and to relate to the employee named, that the employee began employment on *(month/day/year)* ___/___/___ **and that to the best of my knowledge the employee is eligible to work in the United States. (State employment agencies may omit the date the employee began employment.)**

Signature of Employer or Authorized Representative	Print Name	Title
Business or Organization Name	Address *(Street Name and Number, City, State, Zip Code)*	Date *(month/day/year)*

Section 3. Updating and Reverification. To be completed and signed by employer.

A. New Name *(if applicable)*	B. Date of rehire *(month/day/year) (if applicable)*

C. If employee's previous grant of work authorization has expired, provide the information below for the document that establishes current employment eligibility.

Document Title:_____   Document #:_____   Expiration Date (if any):___/___/___

I attest, under penalty of perjury, that to the best of my knowledge, this employee is eligible to work in the United States, and if the employee presented document(s), the document(s) I have examined appear to be genuine and to relate to the individual.

Signature of Employer or Authorized Representative	Date *(month/day/year)*

Form I-9 (Rev. 11-21-91)N Page 2

Worksheet #26

Making Direct Contact

1. Ask for the name of the person who hires employees *and write it down.*

    _____

    _____

    _____

2. Ask to speak to that person.

    _____

    _____

    _____

3. Ask if there is a job open.

    _____

    _____

    _____

If yes, ask for an appointment.

    _____

    _____

    _____

If no, ask when they will be hiring.

    _____

    _____

    _____

Ask if they know anyone else who is hiring now.

    _____

    _____

    _____

Worksheet #27

Hidden Job Market

Job Lead Script

Hello, my name is (first and last name) _____.

I was referred to you by Mr./Mrs./Ms. (correct first and last name) _____.

I understand that your company is hiring for (name position). Do you have a few minutes to talk with me about the job?

If the employee doesn't want to talk, tell them you are sorry to disturb them and ask if there is a better time to call. Thank them for their time and then hang up.

Can you tell me a little about that position? Can you tell me the name of the person doing the hiring or a contact name? _____

Are you happy with your company? _____

Can I mention that I have talked to you? _____

If the employee gives you a contact, don't prolong the call.

You've been very helpful. Thank you, Mr./Mrs./Ms. _____.

This method is worth a try. It can work well, but it depends on the person who referred you to this employee and their relationship. It may be a foot in the door. Jobs are filled very quickly, so follow up with any contacts you are given as soon as possible.

See how many job leads you can pick up in a week.

Worksheet #28

Employer Contact Worksheet

Date	Company	Phone	Hiring Person	Openings	Contact Person	Call Back

Worksheet #29

Teamwork

We don't always stop to think how many team members it takes to do a job.

Look at the list of jobs below. What teamwork does the job require? Write an example of teamwork next to each job.

Job   **Teamwork**

Chef _____

Waitress _____

Car salesperson _____

Cashier _____

Delivery driver _____

Janitor _____

Stocker _____

Courtesy clerk _____

Lobby person _____

Hotel housekeeper _____

Pizza maker _____

Napkin roller _____

Construction worker _____

Computer programmer _____

Data entry clerk _____

Dishwasher _____

Manager _____

Security guard _____

Nurse _____

Bartender _____

Teacher _____

Assembly worker _____

Write a job that you have worked. It can be paid or volunteer.

_____

Did it require teamwork?   Yes   No

Draw a picture of your team. Use stick figures. Circle your part.

What part did you play on this team?

_____

Did you enjoy working on your team?   Yes   No

Why or why not?

_____

_____

Worksheet #30

Roles in the Workplace

Give three answers to each question.

1. Why would the manager be hired to oversee company profits and policies?

   _____

   _____

   _____

2. Why would the assistant manager be concerned about supporting the manager, especially if he or she disagrees with the manager?

   _____

   _____

   _____

3. Why would the long-term employee be proud of his or her job performance? After being there so long, who cares?

   _____

   _____

   _____

4. Why would the unhappy camper even have anything to say? Why not just quit?

   _____

   _____

   _____

5. Why would a person be a floater?

   _____

   _____

   _____

Worksheet #31

Where Do I Fit?

List where each member of the team fits.

Step 1

Manager/owner: _____

Assistant manager: _____

Long-time employee: _____

Unhappy camper: _____

Floater: _____

Step 2

Manager/owner: _____

Assistant manager: _____

Long-time employee: _____

Unhappy camper: _____

Floater: _____

Step 3

Manager/owner: _____

Assistant manager: _____

Long-time employee: _____

Unhappy camper: _____

Floater: _____

Worksheet #32

Knowing Yourself

Look back over your workbook sheets. Check all the things in the list below that describe you. These are some of your selling points.

Head

_____ Good student

_____ Good problem solver

_____ Good eyesight

_____ Good listener

_____ Good speller

_____ Good at explaining myself

_____ Night person

_____ Day person

Arms and Hands

_____ Physically strong

_____ Can lift heavy objects

_____ Coordinated

_____ Good with my hands

_____ Good dexterity (fingers)

_____ Write well

Legs and Feet

_____ Strong legs

_____ Bend easily

_____ Stand for long periods of time

_____ Sit for long periods of time

_____ Do running sports

_____ Exercise a lot

_____ Can bike fast

_____ Can walk fast

_____ Good dancer

Draw a picture putting your body parts together.

Worksheet #33

Writing Promotional Ads

Write an Ad About Someone

Talk with a partner and then write an ad about them. The ad should mention your partner's interests, skills, and selling points.

_____

_____

_____

_____

_____

_____

_____

Write an Ad About Yourself

Now write an ad about yourself, mentioning your interests, skills, and selling points.

_____

_____

_____

_____

_____

_____

_____

This ad is going to run in the *Wall Street Journal*. Each word will cost $100. Go back over your own ad. Mark out any words that you can eliminate without losing your selling points.

Worksheet #34

Differences Between School and the Workplace

✔ In school, counselors and teachers are paid to do a job. That job is to help prepare you for success.

✔ In school, decisions are around you and sometimes involve you.

✔ In school, everyone wants you to succeed and tries hard to help you.

✔ In school, you are surrounded by people who have common backgrounds and common problems and interests.

✔ In school, if you do not work, you get disciplined—but you are also encouraged to do better.

✔ In the workplace, you are paid to do a job. You do it or you will not succeed.

✔ In the workplace, nobody cares about your decisions. Everything revolves around management and the company.

✔ In the workplace, most people don't care if you succeed. You have to do it on your own. In fact, some of your co-workers may not want you to succeed.

✔ In the workplace, there may be no one who has the same problems or interests as you.

✔ In the workplace, if you do not work, you get fired.

Worksheet #35

How to Keep or Lose a Job

Circle a thumbs-up for a good behavior or a thumbs-down for a bad one.

Good/acceptable		Bad/unacceptable
👍	Using bad language	👎
👍	Working overtime	👎
👍	Breaking safety rules	👎
👍	Fighting	👎
👍	Helping co-workers	👎
👍	Turning in a lost wallet	👎
👍	Using drugs	👎
👍	Carrying a weapon	👎
👍	Working on your day off	👎
👍	Answering the phone politely	👎
👍	Stealing	👎
👍	Talking with friends on the phone	👎
👍	Being on time	👎
👍	Wearing clean clothes	👎
👍	Drinking alcohol	👎
👍	Making the boss look good	👎
👍	Having a good attitude	👎
👍	Talking back	👎
👍	Refusing to do a job	👎
👍	Lying on an application	👎
👍	Being cooperative and friendly	👎

Worksheet #36

Behaviors That Will Get You Fired

Most people don't get fired over big things, like stealing, cheating, and fighting. You know that these kinds of behaviors will get you fired. However, small problems can also cause you to be fired. They are the kind of things that occur daily—things you are used to getting away with in school, at home, and with friends. You could cost the company money if you continue these behaviors in the workplace.

Why would these things get you fired? Write a reason next to each behavior.

Clocking in early _____

Lying about being late _____

Personal calls _____

Attitude _____

Gossiping_____

Jealousy _____

Bad-mouthing the boss _____

Doing sloppy work _____

Being too slow _____

Breaking rules _____

Taking too many breaks _____

Not multi-tasking _____

Smoking in restricted areas _____

Worksheet #37

Interview Tips

Good Verbal Cues

✔ Use your power words in your interview.

✔ Make sure you understand the questions you are asked.

✔ Think of something you have accomplished or succeeded in doing that you can relate to the job you are applying for.

✔ Speak clearly—don't mumble.

✔ Try to ask early in the interview what kind of person they are looking for. (You are that person.)

✔ A pause before you speak is sometimes effective and helps you relax.

✔ Try hard to be genuine and honest in your answers. Make your voice sound sincere.

✔ Ask one or two questions.

✔ Ask for the job!

✔ Try to pin down when the decision will be made.

✔ Ask permission to call the interviewer if you have not heard by a predetermined time.

✔ Thank the interviewer for his or her time and for the opportunity to have the interview.

Good Nonverbal Cues

✔ Wear clothes that are neat and clean. Be well-groomed.

✔ Have clean hair and nails.

✔ Women should not have chipped nail polish.

✔ Men should be cleanly shaven (or with beards neatly trimmed and clean) and wear polished shoes.

✔ Sit up straight in the chair. Don't slouch.

✔ Look the interviewer in the eyes (or the nose if you prefer).

✔ Plant your feet firmly on the floor. This will keep you from fidgeting.

✔ Keep your hands in your lap and away from your face.

✔ Smile occasionally. It will make you feel better.

Worksheet #38

Interview Questions

These are questions most employers will ask at one time or another:

Tell me about yourself.

What do you like to do for fun?

Do you know what a _____ does?

Are you available to work weekends?

Have you had any experience in _____ ?

Tell me about your job experience.

What did you like about that job?

What did you not like about that job?

Is transportation a problem?

On a scale of one to ten, how would you rate yourself on responsibility?

How many days of school did you miss last year?

Did you fill out the application by yourself?

If I called one of your teachers, what would he or she say about you?

Why do you want to work for this company?

What kind of salary are you looking for?

This job is very fast-paced. Will that be a problem for you?

When can you start?

Worksheet #39

20 Points to Remember in Job Hunting

1. You have done more than you think. Memorize your power words!

2. Most jobs are not in the paper. Ask people you know about jobs where they work or call employers directly.

3. You have to be able to tell an employer what you can do and why you want the job.

4. Write your resume before you start looking for a job. Then take it with you.

5. Fill out the application form very carefully. Don't leave any blanks. Don't tell any lies.

6. Follow up with the employer after you fill out an application.

7. Have clean hair and clean, neat clothes when you go to an interview.

8. When you meet an employer, shake his or her hand.

9. Speak clearly in the interview; don't mumble.

10. Show the employer you are interested in the job by asking questions.

11. Tell the employer your strengths—good grades, good attendance, good attitude, whatever you think will help.

12. Tell the employer your job objectives.

13. Don't talk about what you want to do *after* this job. Let the employer know you will stay at the job.

14. Find out about what the company does *before* an interview.

15. Look at the interviewer's nose when you answer questions. It's easier than looking him or her in the eye.

16. When ending the interview, let the employer know you want the job.

17. Say thank you for the interview before you leave. Then send a thank-you note.

18. Be at work on time and every day.

19. Don't blame other people for your mistakes.

20. Make your boss look good!

Worksheet #40

Interview Checklist

	Good	Acceptable	Comments
Appearance			
Clothes			
Jewelry			
Hair			
Speaking			
Loud enough/too loud			
Clear			
Uses power words			
Says thank you			
Asks for the job			
Other			
Smiles			
Sits straight			
Shakes hands			
Looks at the interviewer's face			

The Final Step

Interview Self-Test

I know my six power words.   Yes   No

List them:

1. _____

2. _____

3. _____

4. _____

5. _____

6. _____

I know my short-term goals.   Yes   No

List them:

_____

_____

_____

_____

I know my long-term goals.   Yes   No

List them:

_____

_____

_____

_____

I know whether I am a negative or positive person.   Yes   No

Which are you?   Positive   Negative

I know my personal barriers.   Yes   No

List them:

1. _____

2. _____

3. _____

4. _____

I know how to write a resume.   Yes   No
Is it past, present, or future? Circle one.

I know how to write a cover letter.   Yes   No
Is it past, present, or future? Circle one.

I know how to fill out an application.   Yes   No
Is it past, present, or future? Circle one.

I know how to use a JIST Card.   Yes   No

I am prepared to answer interview questions.   Yes   No

I am prepared to ask interview questions.   Yes   No

I know what will get me fired.   Yes   No

I am prepared for the interview.   Yes   No

I am prepared for an unexpected question.   Yes   No

Congratulations! You are job smart!

Advanced Worksheets

Some of the worksheets in this section are designed for students who can accept more challenging exercises requiring less instructor involvement. These sheets are arranged in numerical and step sequence. (You can easily tell an advanced worksheet by the letter *a* that follows the worksheet number.) Please keep in mind that there is not always a corresponding advanced worksheet for every worksheet activity. Also, some of the advanced worksheets may be used with the entire class. However, it is up to the instructor to determine when and how to use these advanced worksheets in the classroom.

Worksheet #2a

Identifying Principles

Things I Would Not Do/Things I Might Do

Read the following list. Print an N in the blank next to things you would not do. Print an M in the blank next to things you might do.

_____ Walk away from an accident

_____ Report someone for stealing

_____ Make excuses for not showing up

_____ Make fun of people

_____ Tell someone they are dumb

_____ Hit someone at work

_____ Hit a good friend

_____ Visit with friends at work

_____ Take something from work

_____ Make long-distance phone calls from work

_____ Punch a time card for a friend

_____ Take money from the cash register

_____ Pretend to read well

_____ Tell lies about a co-worker

_____ Deny a mistake

_____ Drive someone's car without permission

_____ Steal someone's clothes and lie about it

_____ Create an "accident" on purpose

_____ Tell a stranger my address

_____ Hitchhike

_____ Get into a car with a stranger

_____ Lie to a police officer

_____ Lie on an application

_____ Brag frequently

_____ Walk out at work

_____ Tell a dirty joke

_____ Steal money

_____ Eat on the job

_____ Do drugs

_____ Drink alcohol

_____ Wear dirty clothes

_____ Go through someone's coat pockets

_____ Repeat gossip

_____ Eat someone else's food

_____ Take a lot of breaks

_____ Carry a gun

____ Carry a knife   ____ Tell a secret

____ Kick a neighbor's dog   ____ Cuss someone out

____ Pinch a baby   ____ Slip out of the house

____ Tell on a friend   ____ Fake being sick

____ Break into a house   ____ Drive without a driver's license

____ Break a promise

Count your Ns. These are *your principles.* Look over your list. What do your Ns tell you about yourself? Are you kind? Are you honest? Are you neat? Responsible? Your Ns will tell you.

In the space below, write a few lines describing your principles (what your Ns say about you).

_____

_____

_____

_____

_____

_____

_____

_____

_____

Worksheet #4a

My Interests

Read the following list of interests and circle what you think is fun:

Watching TV	Listening to or playing music
Using the VCR	Watching movies
Shopping	Playing sports
Looking at art	Looking at Web sites
Doing puzzles	Reading
Fixing motors	Driving cars/reading about cars
Baking	Cooking
Using a computer	Cleaning
Using makeup	Sightseeing
Going to concerts	Taking care of animals
Being with family	Going to church
Camping	Going to holiday gatherings
Acting	Singing
Dancing	Taking care of plants

What kinds of things interest you? Think of two things you are interested in. Why do these things interest you? When did you start being interested in them? How much time do you spend on these interests? In the space below, write a few sentences about why you are interested in these things.

_____

_____

Now spend a few minutes thinking about what kinds of jobs you are interested in. Are there any similarities between the jobs that interest you and your hobbies? Can you think of any ways to use your hobbies or interests in a job? In the space below, write down ideas on how you can use your interests in a job.

_____

_____

Worksheet #6a

My Skills

Read the following list of skills and circle what you can do:

Add numbers	Grow plants	Use a computer
Explain things	Sing	Cut the lawn
Ride a bike	Clean	Play volleyball
Assemble things	Paint	Use the telephone
Fix motors	Skate	Dance
Run	Cook	Read
Search the Internet	Send e-mail	Write
Baby-sit	Play an instrument	Draw
Give customer service	Type	Read music
Sew	Cut hair	Other: _____
Build things	Play basketball	Other: _____

Pick one skill that you enjoy using. In the space below, write a few lines about how you learned that skill and how you use it. For example, maybe you enjoy adding numbers, you learned the skill in school, and you use the skill to keep your checkbook balanced.

_____

_____

_____

Now think of jobs that might use that skill. Write them in the space below.

_____

_____

_____

Worksheet #8a

Setting Goals for Me

There are two questions you need to ask yourself before setting short-term and long-term goals:

1. What do you want to do as a career (job)?

2. What do you want your career (job) to do for you?

On the line below, write your ideal career.

_____

Now list all the things you want this career to do for you.

Example: Buy a car

_____

_____

_____

_____

What goals are you setting to make this happen?

6 months	12 months	5 years

Worksheet #9a

Charting Your Personal Voyage

It is important to have a good idea of where you want to go before you leave on a trip. There is an old saying that goes like this: "If you don't know where you're going, chances are you won't get there!"

Look at the table below. For each item listed down the side, think about where you want to be in 6 months, 12 months, and 5 years. These are your goals. Where do you want to be living in 6 months? How will you be getting to work in 12 months? How much money will you be making in 5 years? List your goals beside each item in the columns below.

	6 months	**12 months**	**5 years**
Location			
Housing			
Transportation			
Finances			
Relationships			
Health			
Education			
Extra goal:			
Extra goal:			

Worksheet #12a

Check Your Attitude

Pick a time every day, either in the morning or in the evening, and check your attitude on this worksheet for that day. Be honest—you need to know. If you aren't feeling happy or sad, write a word for what you are feeling in the Other column. Do this for one week.

	Happy	Sad	Other
Sunday			
Monday			
Tuesday			
Wednesday			
Thursday			
Friday			
Saturday			

When you have finished filling in every day, look back over the sheet. Were you usually happy? Sad? Angry? Think about your attitude and how it reflects upon you in the workplace.

Worksheet #13a

Make a Quick Fix

What works as an "attitude fixer" for you? Circle the things that might perk you up if you were in a bad mood.

Talking to friends	Watching videos	Watching sports	Listening to music	Going to church
Playing team sports	Singing	Doing artwork	Doing crafts	Working puzzles
Playing video games	Taking a walk	Riding a bike	Taking a drive	Going to the city
Going to a special event	Writing a letter	Writing a story	Dancing	Swimming
Taking a sauna	Working out	Jogging	Skating	Skiing
Taking a shower	Planning a trip	Partying with friends	Eating in a restaurant	Snacking
Going shopping	Buying something	Talking to family	Reading a book	Playing games

Now go back and compare the things you circled. Which five things would change your bad attitude the fastest? In the spaces below, write the five things you chose.

1. _____

2. _____

3. _____

4. _____

5. _____

Now you know five things that can change your attitude from bad to good. The next time you are having a bad day, go back over this list and plan to do some of these five things. Nothing is too silly if it works for you. Remember, your attitude is yours to change!

Worksheet #15a

I Shall Overcome

Spend a few minutes thinking about your barriers. Then answer the questions below.

1. What are your barriers to the career or job you want?

    _____

    _____

2. Why are they barriers?

    _____

    _____

3. List three things you can do about these barriers.

    _____

    _____

4. List three famous people who had employment barriers.

    _____

    _____

5. What did they do to overcome their barriers?

    _____

    _____

Look at the list of barriers below. Do you know anyone who has one of these barriers who is working in a job? Can you think of a job someone with each of these barriers can do? In the space beside each barrier, write the job.

Deafness _____

Blindness _____

Uses a wheelchair _____

Attention Deficit/Hyperactivity Disorder _____

Reading disability _____

Epilepsy _____

Diabetes _____

Speech impairment _____

Worksheet #21a

Sample JIST Cards

Below are two sample JIST Cards. Read through them and then answer the questions on the next page.

Shelly Barton
E-mail: sbarton@hotmail.com

Home: (512) 555-7608
Message: (512) 555-7465

Position Desired: General Office/Clerical

Skills: More than two years of work experience plus one year of training in office practices. Trained in word processing and electronic spreadsheets; post general ledger; handle payables, receivables, and most accounting tasks. Good interpersonal skills; get along with most people. Can meet deadlines and handle pressure well.

Desire career-oriented position; will relocate.

Organized, honest, reliable, and hard-working.

Stephen Voorhees

Home: (312) 555-8396
Cell phone: (312) 555-6497

Job Objective: Sales/Counter Clerk

Skills: One year of experience working part-time as a counter clerk in a fast-food restaurant. Operated cash register and served customers. Graduate of school-to-work transition course. Classes in business and math. Work well with others; good team worker.

Willing to work any hours.

Friendly, honest, hard-working, dependable.

---

1. What does each card tell you about the person who wrote it?

   _____

   _____

   _____

2. What are Shelly Barton's power words?

   _____

   _____

   _____

3. What are Stephen Voorhees's power words?

   _____

   _____

   _____

4. Can you find any negatives in these cards?

   _____

   _____

   _____

5. If you were an employer, would you want to interview either of these people?

   _____

   _____

   _____

Worksheet #22a

JIST Card Worksheet

Complete each of the sections below. Your answers will give you all the information you need to complete a JIST Card of your own.

Your Name:_____

List your complete, formal name here (not your nickname).

Your Phone Number: _____

E-mail Address (optional): _____

Second Phone Number (optional): _____

List a second phone number here if you have one. This could be a cell phone or the number of a reliable friend or family member who will take messages for you.

Job Objective: _____

List the job objective you wrote for your resume.

Skills: _____

_____

_____

Include your education, any work experience and accomplishments, and skills you have learned on the job.

Preferred Working Conditions (optional): _____

_____

_____

This is where you can list any special advantages you offer or preferences you have. For example, will you work second or third shift? Will you relocate? Do you want to work in a fast-paced environment?

Your Power Words: _____

_____

_____

This is where you list your six power words, the things that make you a valuable employee.

Worksheet #24a

Working Papers

Read each question carefully and circle the correct answer.

1. **Which form do you fill out to tell the government how much money to withhold from your check in taxes?**

    I-9 form   resume   W-4 form

2. **Which form lets the employer know you are either a U.S. citizen or have the proper permits to work here?**

    driver's license   application   I-9 form

3. **Where do you go to replace a lost Social Security card?**

    Library   Post Office   Social Security Office

4. **Can you just tell an employer your Social Security number as proof of identification?**

    yes   no

5. **What can you use for identification if you don't have a driver's license?**

    state photo ID card   application   birth certificate

6. **Can you use a credit card to prove identification?**

    yes   no

7. **If you are single, how many dependents can you claim on your W-4 form?**

    1   2   0

8. **Your references should be people who have known you for at least how long?**

    5 years   1 year   since you were born

9. **Can you refuse to fill out a W-4 form?**

    yes   no   sometimes

10. **What should you do if you are asked to sign a form you don't understand?**

    refuse   sign it   ask someone to explain it to you first

Worksheet #26a

My Networking Groups

In the left-hand column below, list as many groups as you can think of that you can contact for help in your job search. Examples might be students at your school, your teachers, people at your church or synagogue, and members of your sports team. In the right-hand column, list a key person from each group you can talk to.

Group	Key Person
1. Family	
2. Friends	
3.	
4.	
5.	
6.	
7.	
8.	
9.	
10.	

Worksheet #27a

Job Hunting Online and Off

Use the Internet or the library to look for job openings three times this week. Here are some Web sites and other resources you can use to search for jobs in your area that fit your skills and interests. You can also use a search engine to find Web sites focused on local employment information.

Web sites for job searching

- ✔ www.monster.com
- ✔ www.flipdog.com
- ✔ www.careerbuilder.com
- ✔ www.hotjobs.com
- ✔ www.ajb.dni.us

Other useful resources

- ✔ State and local government agencies
- ✔ Local radio stations
- ✔ Private employment agency Web sites
- ✔ www.careeroink.com

Below, list five job opportunities you found on the Internet or at the library.

1. _____
2. _____
3. _____
4. _____
5. _____

Worksheet #28a

Telemarketing Script

Working from your list, begin contacting employers. To get a job interview, you must get an invitation from the person who makes the hiring decision. That person is usually the manager of the department in which you want to work. Keep in mind that **the human resources department does not have the ultimate power to hire.** Try to secure the name of the manager. One way to get an interview is to call and set up an appointment. The following script might be used when setting up an appointment.

The conversation should be completed in 30 to 40 seconds. Be friendly, be enthusiastic, and speak clearly.

1. **Ask for the manager of the department by name. If the manager is not available when you call, ask if there is a good time to call again.**

   "Hello, may I speak with _____?"

2. **When talking to the manager, briefly introduce yourself.**

   "Hello, _____ . My name is _____."

3. **Make a brief, friendly statement.**

   "I appreciate your taking time to talk with me," or "How are you doing this morning?"

4. **Make a direct statement or give the reason for the call.**

   "I am a recent graduate from _____. I am looking for a position as a _____. I feel I have the qualifications to do this job, and I have a strong interest in working for your company. May I set up an appointment with you to discuss my qualifications?" (You may have an opportunity to use your power words.)

5. **If there are no positions open, ask for a referral.**

   "Can you suggest other companies I can contact that might be interested in someone with my skills?"

6. **Make your closing statement.**

   If the interview was granted, "Great! That is _____ sharp on _____. Thank you very much. I'm looking forward to meeting you in person."

   If the interview was not granted, "Thank you for your time. May I call again at a later date, maybe in six weeks, when job opportunities might be better? Thank you, _____. Remember, my name is _____."

Worksheet #29a

Teams

The word *team* refers to any group organized to work together. Let's take a look at a very simple team structure from the workplace.

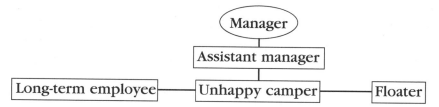

This team is organized to work together to make a profit for the company. That is the goal. The reward is a paycheck.

Make a list of teams you have been part of at work; at school; and in your community, church, or family. Maybe you worked on a "team" to clean out the garage at home, plan a party, or complete a job.

_____

_____

_____

Choose one team experience and draw a diagram in the space below of that team. (Look at the diagram of the workplace team for an example.)

Why was this team organized? What was the goal? What was the reward?

_____

_____

_____

Worksheet #30a

People We Recognize in the Workplace

Can you unscramble the words in the first column to match the words in the second column? Draw a line from the word in the first column to the matching word in the second column.

SIGPOS	ASSISTANT MANAGER
GNLO ETRM OMELPEYE	COMPLAINER
IRLA	GRIPER
GMNEARA	UNHAPPY CAMPER
TLAETTLEAT	KNOW-IT-ALL
PLCOAIMERN	GOSSIP
LOARFTE	FLOATER
HROCUG	CLOWN
ZYAL	JOKER
LEKART	GOODY TWO SHOES
YHPAPNU PCRMAE	LIAR
DYOOG WTO HSSEO	MANAGER
RPREGI	JERK
NWCOL	LONG-TERM EMPLOYEE
TSASAITNS ANRGMEA	GROUCH
RJKE	TATTLETALE
KREJO	LAZY
WNOK TI LAL	TALKER

Worksheet #32a

Descriptive Power Words 1

You only need a few words to describe yourself when speaking and writing. The more you practice, the better you become at using fewer words to describe something.

Take a few minutes and look at this picture of an office. Write down words that describe the person who has this office. See how many words you can come up with.

_____

_____

_____

_____

Worksheet #33a

Descriptive Power Words 2

Take a few minutes to look again at the picture of the office. Using your list of
words, write a short article for the newspaper describing the owner of this office.
Use as few words as possible.

_____

_____

_____

_____

_____

_____

_____

Now team up with a partner and, using your lists and articles, write an ad about this
person. Each word you use will cost your team $100. See which team can write the
cheapest ad and still describe the person. We will vote on the best ad.

_____

_____

_____

_____

_____

_____

Worksheet #35a

Don't Get Fired!

Some behaviors will get you into trouble at work. Some will get you fired immediately.

Look through the list below. Put a Y beside an item if you think it will get you fired. Put an N if you think it won't get you fired. Put a D if it depends upon the circumstances. (Usually a manager will have to decide.)

_____ Lying

_____ Stealing

_____ Doing someone else's work for them

_____ Calling in sick

_____ Using profanity

_____ Having friends visit you at work

_____ Fighting

_____ Someone turning in complaints on you

_____ Clocking in late

_____ Using the Internet for non-work purposes

_____ Talking back to the boss

_____ Asking questions

_____ Using drugs in the workplace

_____ Someone redoing what you have done

_____ Asking for help

_____ Carrying a weapon

_____ Gossiping

_____ Having alcohol on your breath

_____ Refusing to do a job assignment

_____ Abusing the telephone

_____ Breaking safety rules

_____ Customers complaining about you

_____ Talking about the boss

_____ Having a bad attitude

Now go back through the list and circle the items you think would get you fired immediately.

Worksheet #36a

Climbing the Ladder of Success

You can think of moving up in your job as climbing a ladder. Some steps will take you closer to the top (staying on the job and getting a raise), and some will make you fall to the bottom (being fired).

Look at the list of steps below. Starting with Step 1 on the ladder, write in the steps you think will take you to the top of the ladder to keep your job and get a raise.

	Keeping the job and getting a raise
10	
9	
8	
7	
6	
5	
4	
3	
2	
1	
	Starting the job

Working overtime

Helping co-workers

Leaving work early

Filling in when someone is sick

Working weekends

Refusing to ask for help when I'm confused

Staying away from gossip

Using bad language

Making personal calls from work

Being friendly

Carrying a weapon to work

Staying late to finish a job

Talking behind my boss's back

Not missing work

Being on time

Smelling of alcohol

Gossiping

Horsing around with co-workers

Answering the phone politely

Asking for help when I'm confused

Dating a co-worker

Dating my boss

Having a good attitude

Smiling

Being late frequently

Saying please and thank you

Worksheet #37a

Step-by-Step to the Interview

Look at the list of steps below. Number the steps in order. For example, if the first thing you do is write down the date and time of the interview, then put a 1 by that step, and so on.

Remember: Luck is where opportunity and preparation cross.

_____ Eat breakfast

_____ Get your resume in order

_____ Write down the date and time of the interview

_____ Be polite to the first person who welcomes you (the receptionist)

_____ Check the clothes you are going to wear; make sure they are clean and pressed

_____ Check your shoes and stockings; make sure your shoes are clean and there are no runs in your stockings

_____ Check the location and address of the interview

_____ Check your transportation and find out how long it will take to get to the interview

_____ Check your alarm clock

_____ Be ready for the interview when you enter the building

_____ Review your interviewing notes

_____ Wash your hair; check cosmetics and deodorant

_____ Be sure you know the interviewer's name and how to pronounce it

Worksheet #38a

Asking and Answering Interview Questions

Key words

For each example, write some key words that would impress an employer for these job seekers to use when answering interview questions.

Gordon is interviewing for a warehouse job. One of his duties is working the forklift. _____

_____

Diane is interviewing for a waitress job at a very expensive restaurant. _____

_____

Christine is interviewing for a data entry job. _____

_____

Dominic is interviewing for a lawn worker position. _____

_____

Roberta is interviewing to be a dry cleaning laundry clerk. _____

_____

Lawrence is interviewing for a security guard position._____

_____

Jeremiah is interviewing for an assembly job. _____

_____

Susie is interviewing at a dress boutique. _____

_____

Asking Appropriate Questions

The questions you ask are as important as the questions you answer. Let's look at some common questions.

Would you ask these questions? Circle Yes or No.

1.	When do my benefits start?	Yes	No
2.	Do I get a vacation the first year?	Yes	No
3.	How many breaks do I get each day?	Yes	No
4.	When do I get a raise?	Yes	No
5.	If I am sick, who do I call?	Yes	No
6.	If my car won't start, who do I call?	Yes	No
7.	If I miss my bus, who do I call?	Yes	No
8.	Can I wear jeans to work?	Yes	No
9.	How many days of work can I miss?	Yes	No

Questions I Should Ask

Write some good questions to ask during an interview.

1. _____

2. _____

3. _____

4. _____

Worksheet #39a

20 Points to Remember in Job Hunting

Review the 20 points here. Then answer the questions at the end of the exercise.

1. **You have done more than you think.** You have used skills you did not recognize; you have values you hold and interests that have become a part of your life. Pick two skills, two principles, and two interests. Learn to express them quickly and clearly. *Memorize your power words!*

2. **Most jobs are not advertised.** The best way to find job openings is to contact companies directly and network with people you know.

3. **Jobs go to people who can communicate their qualifications and show genuine enthusiasm.** People hire people they like. Practice your interviewing skills.

4. **Write your resume early in your job search.** It will help you with your application, paper work, and interviewing techniques.

5. **The application form is very important.** Give it the respect it deserves. It can keep you from getting the interview. If you are hired, it becomes a permanent part of your file. Do not leave any blanks. *Do not tell any lies!*

6. **Follow up with the employer after you have submitted your application.** Be polite but be persistent and try to get an answer.

7. **Appearance is very important in a job interview.** You only have one chance to make a good impression. You don't have to spend money for new clothes, but your clothes must be clean, pressed, and appropriate for the interview. You must have a well-scrubbed look.

8. **A handshake is a polite, proper icebreaker.** It should be firm but not painful.

9. **The interview is a two-way conversation.** It is your opportunity to tell an employer about yourself and to ask questions about the job and the company. *Do not mumble.*

10. **Show an interest in the job.** Show an interest in helping the employer. It shows a willingness to do more. Ask a few questions. It shows you are interested.

11. **Stress your strengths. If your grades are fair to good, say so.** If your attendance is good, say so. If you have participated in school activities, say so. If you participate in sports, say so.

12. **Tell the employer your job objectives.** Make them clear, but be open to change.

13. **Mention future plans only if appropriate.** Your plans must make you appear to be an asset to the employer. Don't spend a lot of time telling the employer what you want to do after this job.

14. **Gather information about the job and the company.** Do your homework to give yourself a head start.

15. **Look your interviewer squarely in the nose.** It's easier than looking him or her in the eye and he or she will never know.

16. **When ending the interview, ask for the job.** You don't have to say, "Pretty please, I want the job." You can be very persuasive in your own manner and style.

17. **Thank the employer for his or her time.** Follow up with a thank-you note.

18. **Be at work consistently and on time.** You cannot be a good employee if you are always late or miss work often. Regardless of the reason, your skills will not carry you if you are not reliable. Tell yourself, "I will always be there. I will always be on time."

19. **Take responsibility for your own actions.** *You are responsible for yourself.*

20. **Remember, employers are mostly concerned about themselves.** If you make them look bad, they will find a way to let you go. If you make them look good, they will try in every way to keep you as an employee and help you up the ladder. If you do not remember anything else, remember this: *Make your boss look good.*

Write your answers to the following questions in the blanks below.

1. Which of your power words would you use to quickly describe what you can do?

   _____

   _____

2. What information should you carry with you so that you can fill out applications completely and correctly?

   _____

   _____

3. How might you carry this information with you (without having to carry your resume around all the time)?

   _____

4. How can you organize your leads so you don't forget to follow up?

   _____

   _____

5. What are some questions you can ask an employer?

   _____

   _____

6. Can you describe your job objective in one or two sentences? Write it here.

   _____

   _____

7. How can you find out about a company before an interview?

   _____

   _____

8. What is the best way to follow up after an interview?

   _____

9. List some times in a new job when you should ask for help.

   _____

   _____

10. List four things you can do to make your boss look good.

   _____

   _____

Worksheet #40a

Interview Checklist

Complete the checklist for each interview you watch.

	Good	Acceptable	Comments
Appearance			
Clothes			
Shoes			
Stockings			
Jewelry			
Purse			
Briefcase			
Glasses			
Hairstyle			
Verbal			
Speaks at good volume			
Speaks clearly			
Sounds sincere			
Gives straight answers			
Uses power words			
States accomplishments			
Asks for the job			
Asks when the decision will be made			
Thanks the interviewer			
Nonverbal			
Smiles			
Has good posture			
Shakes hands			
Uses good hand gestures			
Has a pleasant expression			
Makes eye contact			

Notes